Rhythms of Existence

By

Robin Ouzman Hislop

4

Metopes (i)

(we sleep on air)

time is the demi urge
on the avalanche of now
we sleep on air
like swifts
on flight to distant skies

/Vettone/

if i were a Vettone
you would not pass through this plateau
if you came from outside

everything
this side of the south mountain is ours
you from the north are not welcome

unless you bring

your bulls to water at our river side
we do not fear your fierce charge
here we are always waiting

here we command the rock
that makes the sun & moon bow down
to our river's source comes the mighty porpoise
whose snout is turned to stone

& high on this altar view to that far cleft of hill
rests the boulder that holds the sky down still
& where none may enter without our knowing

/Unfinished poem/

she caught me in her fatal flare
transfixing me with her stare
on air
to bewitch me in her snare
what we did between here & there
i left by the front & she by the stair
seeming to vanish into thin air ......

Casanova lived & died under
the fixed stars with the elegant sperm
that animated a mechanical marionette
as time flowed back into his loins

he liked the cities bright lights & ladies
his greatest fear was to fall off
at the end of the world
but most of all he liked macaroni

/Helen/

return to a false harbour
where ships come in
& their backwaters
never let you leave
not even the rats
only your face remains
fixed lips that cannot speak
          what befell you
a fate that drowned
the heart of the world
where its frenzied cry
beat beneath blind stars
blind eyes turned upon them
though they winked
          as if upon a certainty
yet were inexplicable
like your trapped face
upon the page
beyond reach beyond touch
beyond let me begin
beyond futility

/Litter/

in the noonday sun
on this dumping ground
of the litter of the day
and the litter of our words
in their blind array
we emerge from our autism
as hunter gatherers
into this history of story tellers

& the present fiction of its collective myth
where only our rubbish will outlast us
taking longer to decompose
until plastic jelly fish
emerge from the sea
what's this rubbish they'll say
nothing to eat
but the relics of our forbearers
we'll have to eat our babies!!

We door mice in the stars
but common parlance shan't
be bartered for a bitch - that
is to say that - better a hitch
on the milky way than desert

      Sand   - made to eat each
      day as grail grain - we too
      can peek-a-boo the flossy
      lot of far *aways* and chase
      into darken through night's

            Tunnels singing out its barren
            closures of centuries we have
            bitten on the champ – any of us
            door mice in the stars – perchance!

/The Drifter's Escape/

Proudly the vessel sets forth
from the soft firm shore
mast erect sail full blown
streamers flowing in the wind
into the wine dark sea

Before the tumult the whirlwind spray
the storm blast the lightning strike
the echo in the abyss the shattered
fragments exploded onto tomorrow's shore
the drifts where naked feet   stoop

/Millennium/

i dream of a possible millennium utopia
as i seem to see
a hearse disappear over a hill
the like the band of the illfated in the Seventh Seal
& hear Orpheus's lyre
as his head floats downstream
            in it's song of defiance – perhaps

we are not to blame for our bondage
our confusion   i do not see the world
                      in a grain of sand
but of us as very small in the desert
where we stumble towards its mirage oasis
as freedom within our grasp

& fall into the abyss of delusion
                      so i say again
let the deserts be green once more
& do not hunt the whale in the ocean

/Purple Lilies/

Purple lilies grew so few
i picked them by the seasons for you
i should have counted them too
had i known they were as the lilies grew

if this is a time before we part
it is just an epitaph of a poet's heart
that nothing really ever remains
except the memories of the pain

that life is strange that life is weird
it was a reality that never appeared
it was a theft it was a joke
it was a dream that never awoke

a quantum leap in time
is other than a straight line
this verse is neither symbol nor sign
but merely a curvature of its rhyme

/Aviary/

in this scene
i could be just a pixel
on a screen
a fractal an algorithm simulated
on a quantum computer
& replayed in the year
five thousand & something

think that all the birds in the air
were once Dinosaurs
down the footsteps of time
but isn't it true   i say
we Sapiens once trod through
forests a thousand feet high
with the wild aves
swarming as an aviary
in our flowing hair

/Signatura Rerum/

mother milk mortal moon
pearl of my heart inscribed
entangled in your womb

our spin of light & dim
right left left right
earth born brain divided
in the pond of meaning

the myriad ramifications
reflect anti reflect
our gestalt enframed
           in the language of things

/Woodcutter's Elegy/

Over my defeat only her orbit
you will bring me her heart
when from that high state of grace
you were before
you wept before his impassioned face
before what was shared what was lost
before what had taken place had taken place
& that little trick of fate
the doors that open the doors that close
the doors that wait
within that labyrinthian trap
you cannot escape your state
cast that to the winds that howl by chance
to the fields that wave upon a dance
& judge how you perform before the curtain falls

Metopes (ii)

(a dark amorphous mass)

21

/On the beach/

sex on the beach   a beverage   the addy read
tucked into a snug cove
where we sun our limbs in wicker seats
with seagulls & snorkellers   flipper fins plashing
the glittering sea   white foam breaking chiffon on the rocks

we blip a 1,000 selfies on the jelly roll fleshly
nubile spawning shore
biologically hacked biologically raped
under a celluloid blue sky   buffet on plastic mariscos
before we drift off towards our yellow beige
alabaster domed cupolas
our palatial hotel château to enter its catacombs
bathed in golden light like holographic silhouettes

at night rats will scourge the waterfront promenade
festooning rubbish bins neglected either by
white linen underpaid immigrant blacks from the hotels
or pissed off government employee cleaners

#GOOD NEWS

*New Study / People
eat at least 80,000
plastic particles a year
Story of the week*

i rise from my 5 dollar a day chaisse longe
my 1.50 dollar a day umbrella shade
to float on the see through sea
spitting out those same particles
washed inshore watching brown bits of sewage dirt
through the corners of my eyes

(University of Victoria Canada
who led the research
other foods such as bread
processed products
meat dairy & vegetables
may well contain
just as much plastic)

cluster into filmy layers to coagulate with algae
& mollusc on the rocks that adorn the bay
& tilting my head i look outward
to where the sun will set on a distant isle

/**Colours**/

gray is nobody's colour by fire   gray cloud
the color of the colour of soldiers   gray hair
heralding both blandness and doom   gray teeth
rendered not in white it lingers incognito   gray meme
gray the color each colour hides   gray dream

a pang of mourning for all colours fall   in the theory of gray
                                                   gray wars
are therefore all of life when consumed by shades of   gray
gray plague in this saturated world   gray money
the dampness of dishwater and disappointment
gray god beneath white   gray is every colour
gray gods industry and uniformity   gray emissary
gray people & their dogs
in the wild black-and-white   gray scrub
five hundred colors fade into a once drained leaden sky
a breath of gray beer on the wind   gray joi de vivre
perceives death of trees the death battleships   gray sex
gray apocalypse gloaming its liminal colour   gray
Armageddon
gray meat   gray stew   gray is all theory
because the world into which it is the colour of gray
                                                   is the one
that
                                                   is the one
that

/Wave/

i could be anything
counting the days
what matter the universe
a wave
counting the days
how many breaths

to fill a space
where nobody's saved
that will bring
the next moment
on a wave

waving to a wave
counting the days
on the crest
of a mania
one moment lost
to the next
in an open grave
what matter the universe

 a wave
count them all in
on Noah's
counting the days

what matter the universe
a wave
it's only in time
you count the days
on a throw
into oblivion
keep
one step
ahead of time
counting the days

/From a hospital window/

like a long dead insect
motor cycles in electric windows gleam
as if trying to get on   to get off   a swerve
on the hill   jammed in the valley
houses stacked like egg boxes
cloud & smoke   at the interstices
traffic drone pedestrians cast like shadows
at night   orange electrics
hang out converging symmetries almost ephemerally

i am its inmate   its identity
a dark amorphous mass
turning towards a lighted doorway
to scrawl its signature

a fictitious identity effacing present
with a replaced distance   yonder
where the moment drifts
a wandering mind on a happen stance edge
like light on the sea
an ephemeral instance of memory
a dazzling illusion of tongues
stained with the dust of ages
where i walk on sand
hearing those voices fall over   the horizon of this flat world
the grain of yesterday's tears vanishing in a whirlwind of dust
in multiple dusts   the fumes rage   print the page
we rise with hands of clay   hang the numbers out to dry

                                                        a bag of tricks

/Yahun/

suddenly i flashback to a dangerous
rushing stream tumbling & cold
i remember the water as green   white deep
a slither of a stripped tree trunk straddles
the sheer sided banks which can be crossed
by a few strides & a skip
which all in the bleak grey stone village must do
old or young strong weak or sick
nobody is in sight
the spar looks slippery   shiny
bent with an under-sway to the tug of the flow
a fatal slip & i'm a gonna
but i cross   a few strides & a skip
i come to the first stone dwelling
ground hard & arid   i pass a front dyke
to enter without a door
the burnt earthen floor room in its dim half light

i don't remember how

there's what looks like a built up
large sink made of stone & shingle
& in it half submerged
in clear cold water   small white turnips
it's his only fare   we stare at each other
he is tall thin gaunt with long white hair & beard
clad in a brown home spun gown & cord sandals
he goes to the sink   offers me a soaked turnip

27

is this me in another life time
could i live this life day after day
tonight i will sleep out
i cannot stay   we have not spoken a word
i eat the turnip & leave as suddenly as i came
to a memory which now hinges on a dream
as though a desert wind should move a dune
where you wake to find
what you left behind is beyond you still

/Sex Core/

its pulse drives
the mindless mindful crowd
gravitates it into
automata

into a faceless faced
            phantasmagoria
where multiple saccades
magnetise
erogenous zones

- convert invert revert

regenerate in helpless drift
the machinations of our existence
a suppressed surge - the numbed norm

a dance of marionettes plastered
on glittering billboards
that announce us
their shadows cast into
        rebirth of tomorrow's abyss

relentless the sex core consumes
its victims like sacrificial slaves
led to the slaughter –

as our heads
float by on platters served
the menu of the day – bubble & pop.

/Crowd/

what's my name
in my dream   nightmare really
i'm in a crowd
jostling on all sides
            pressing me with nowhere
            to go
out of controle
        my controle   but i can't help thinking
ants do it so much better
        when suddenly the thought
        hits me

            M Theory

& all this is just a form in my mind
in an infinite universe in space
a curvature of time in my specious present

            & suddenly

there's a surge of panic
rippling through the crowd
like a tsunami
& i want to dial up a number
                on my evolutionary tablet
but i'm just a speck of nothing
in the hollow of the milky way
& the nightmare is a crowd
                in the nightmare

& suddenly

i want to be
                in some green valley
on some ancient Savannah
Far from the Madding Crowd
far from mowed lawns
                potted plants   rubber snakes
                & Micky Mouse toy-land animals

or perhaps i should just
switch on my play station
tune into my simulation
& catch a rocket into outer space

                Headlines
                        corporations are hackers

/Skywards/

under a clear blue sky
                                  naked & alone in my retina
as i lay on my back
                                  the hard ground pressing me
upwards into flight
& where i still hear cries   of distant voices   i am
alone & naked as this sky
beyond its nothingness &
everything   for there is no

                        hiding nor concealment nor
shelter from this loneliness
nor do i know if my heart
                      will cease to beat in the next
instant   i do not know
                      if this is my last breath or if
                      there will be a next after this
& only now under
the naked sky
locked in my retina   i marvel

/Towards Mortality/

he turns his face towards her
Eurydice seems to cling to Orpheus
Eurydice waves farewell to Orpheus
he's turned his face from her

                  all the birds of the air
               swarm in giddying flight

the head of Orpheus
is seared from his neck

               there is a fountain in the air

his head floats down stream

                    Agh   Agh
                    Agh

                here come the piranhas
                flesh seethed from bone

Maenads sing through bloodied lips
& in the cave
Eurydice stands before Hades

            who is shadow itself which darkens

thunder breaks she is deaf
lightning cracks she is blind

/The Art of Deism/

somewhere there's a context
but how did she get there
where did she come from
she's as silent as the grave
but drops a few hints   as
the given structure is now
an abstraction

&

she has already left you
after having created you
through an abstraction
the art of deism   DIY
with whatever tools are
ready to hand   & beat out
     that rhythm on a drum
          je ne regrette rien

/you say & i say/

another bunch of memories
turns up on my doorstep
        dressed in rags
          holding me to ransom
            opting for the highest bidder
i already know tomorrow
will not take flight
                                        save the world with clay balls
nubile women in the sun
signalling a male wilderness
              God is not a poet
Romeo was fourteen Juliet twelve
who wants to live forever
you say tom *a:* to & i say tom *ei* to
          ring a ring of roses we all fall down
            (the village was in quarantine)
              i had a dream last night
              we were all wearing pp masks
              sitting on a bus driving through
            the pearly gates   & God was a poet
          more like a nightmare really
                                        you say & i say

/The Hidden Variable/

when it's off   why even bother
i'm all done   it's just another
it's not on   in what's come
& u can   in what's well
wonder what's gone   well well well
wrong a song   wants to come
on but it's   never to keep
not what fits   bundle to heap
only a bit   but got u
what u ask   through & through
words must pass   an alliterative stash
first & last   in onomatopoeic crash
for a poem   a mere backlash
to be born   mush and mash
beyond the seventh   wonder in zenith

come on soon   the mirage cometh
in a swoon   no doubt about
off's not on   all's in rout
what's gone wrong   we had thieved
a bitty song   to be believed
starts off along   i'm all done
put it away   in what's come
for another day   poem gone astray
it's a play   come what may
the talkie talk   it's off off
or blackboard chalk   just as well
stork & baby   but can't tell
drive me crazy   in fucking hell
that's to begin   off off off
can anyone say   cloud into day
a poem's itness   is its it?

36

/Zombie/

menu of the day zombies v planet   aftermath
octopuses with wings over Atlantis
& today's a bellyful of macro gasoline
in your macro van micro man

algorithms are gonna interiorise cyborgs
between the digital brain & ours
phantom vibrations
insect bot invasion
a slippage in reality
on the spars of dawns unleashed
chip infused rats in the sewers

the information tomb
dust of the milky way

in the deluge of life   the scattered memories
new lives formed   the selves we inhabit
from the strangers we are   to the strangers we will be

& even the mighty Amazon   deep winding creature
devouring jungles in her wake   to lay on her dark bed
heads to oceans that turn to deserts   where satellites play at dice

Metopes (iii)

(the green embedded fissures of our padded cells)

/Even now/

(Beginning of the 1ˢᵗ Lockdown)

now even now
it's like a ghost town now
& O the distant hills

are a more ghostly blue
than before

now even a few stray locals
come & go stranger even now
than they were before &

O the dear police cars patrol
with speakers are more ghostly too

& through my bedroom window
the gable end rock house wall
grows evermore iconic faces

than before   even now
as daily the days flock by
more than before   now even now

/Strange Fruit/

strange fruit in the wet market
a vampire kiss
human blood   human meat

but save the economy not the ecology
surveillance   surveillance   surveillance
monitor our sick brains
& bury the remains in silicon valley

like fallen Caryatids we bear own epitaphs
the hours of the street endure their empathy
with landscapes ordered from the abattoir
"exotic wildlife threatens humans"

cockroach traffic cockroach computers
user friendly amplify & invade
degrade habitats   population growth summons
armament   until   hyssops burst through
the green embedded fissures of our padded cells
& the pavements crack beneath

/Somewhere over /
(coming out of a lockdown)

Oh when the saints   tread tenderly
flora & foliage are abundant   so the pain
with bird song   is not seen   with the
lessening of   in my eyes   human traffic
bury me here *go marching in*   & laugh
in the face of the wind & come back next year
bring me the face
                      somewhere over the rainbow

when will we return?   of *the grateful dead*
i wanna be   & i will sow   *skies are blue*
the flora of tomorrow   will the deserts be green
again   *amongst that number* as when Homo Erectus
trekked through them?   *once in a lullaby*
what did they seek freedom? before confusion
& the babble of tongues   *when the saints go marching in*

/Approach/

approach   approach   approach
alone in my heart
let the day sail away
i shall stay in exultancy
the dust track leads
nowhere   in twilight she disrobes
anywhere's a gradient nowhere
dawn is like this stray dog
two years ago   crying somewhere
they had bulldozed   afraid   lost
their way through this
the local *alcalde* believed
the dust track   it would improve the economy
little did he know elephants return to the wilderness
wilderness wilderness wilderness   leads nowhere

                         in exultancy
                         at great heights
at twilight
the grandeur of the boulders   she disrobes
hovering upon the hillside   alone in my heart
approach   approach   approach
will hurtle down to unfathomable
the day sails   depths
now extends   as we approach   approach   approach

autumnal sludge   trudge mush   trudge mush
dear ape   sweet ape   good ape
O homo rapiens   beautylovedeath
rhapsody in blue minor   the trees
stark & bare   don't care
mush trudge sludge   mush trudge sludge
swing low sweet   swing low sweet
coming for to   coming for to
depending on where of kith of kin of kinship
dear ape   beauty ape   love ape
death gape   in the dark void   sing
beautylovedeath beautylovedeath beautylovedeath
deathbeautylove deathbeautylove deathbeautylove
& so on   in a hole   to fall in fall in fall in
falling   falling   falling
O   O   O   dear ape
time closing the gap   the long trek back
to the track   the track   the track
ancestor of the comet
where walls tremble back & bones stack
in the black in the black in the black
where echoes distort the answer
what stays   what does not leave
in tunnels of light   in tunnels of dark
that cross & intercede   sculptured in the rock
the body on a rack   where words crack
as sound surfaces   on the surf surf surf surf surf

/Out of Africa/

we will never know
the origins of the universe
nor of life
language is never
quite enough   barely sufficient

i walk into the stones
their evanescent landscapes
their iconic dreams

or the dream from the photons
from your eyes
as they become
the phosphenes of the dead stars
in mine

out of Africa back to Africa

                    morning lifts from night the eye
              to amaze the multiplicity of shapes
                    made real where shadows show
at gallows height open light   closed light
                    a shape in an instant of before
         or perhaps far more where time wefts
                    its blaze the property of an event
                    made the reality of now &

                    memories like the shadows haze
                    as if to mould a day of clay
                    to add a little or to take away
                    in a moment of a world held
                    at play with scarcely time enough
                    to say goodbye before decay

/Episodes/

episodes however brief
virus in the slaughterhouses
obedience to the state
or there is fragmentation

surrounded by hegemony
that camouflages our right of way
we multiply in expectancy
to gain the wealth of the world

this is what life has led us to
the unknowable unknowables
    the something and the nothing
            helpless as leaves upon a tree

early morning mist rain
rolls on the blue mountains
this is the realm of exile
where we play with words

the silent absent words
        embedded in every action
before we speak that tell
episodes however brief

/Poems poems poems/

written on wind
who will win
i will not be here

the green man
or green money
our extinction
or a dystopia

or simply a creature
amongst creatures
in the cascade of life

i will not be here
be here be here
do you hear
why should i care

our absurd folly
arms   nations
tyranny of the few

lost trek on the tundra
what does it matter
joker & thief
written on wind

poems poems poems
epitaphs to their tombs
do they open them?

/Over the Traces/

over the traces heaven & hell
hell & heaven   traces so damn
flash   fade   far & near on
                        a sunny day
                        walking the dog
                        sniffing its way
                        tell me if you find it
some hope   shock over & out
trail blazer
width of a band et al.,
can't go on will   drawing comparisons
as if   through analogies
                        like Eskimos & Pygmies
                        should find a common ground
pissed off with fake media
                        blowing up
                        like a balloon
        'pop'
                        into junkadoria
sky lights paraded
                        as if google metopes
on the supermarket's shelves
while XR rebels glue themselves
to the railings   like suffragettes
what my last words might be
& whether they'll be   little black dots
                        in the cloud
paid for in pasta   & where perhaps
                        they may well petrify - over the traces

48

/Homo Erectus/

terror keep while i weep
i stand before you
in the art gallery of time
obliterated
human woman man
what have you done
what have you become
that i am undone
alone as never before

you have harvested my destruction

two million years
you recreate the memory
in which we are
a shadow & an apparition
a reflection on your retina
in which i disappear

/Dementia deterred today/

dementia deterred today
i met a man with a gun
who went where the sky face was
then shot a hole in the sky
where the face of god appeared
which dropped down dead
next to me stood a dog
we went for a walk in the wood
all the people nodded & smiled
the world went up in flame
everybody was up in flame
next to me stood a dog
the people i met nodded
where the face of god appeared
which dropped down
next to nobody
as the world went up in flame
today i met nobody & everybody
who shot a gun & the world smiled
we went to a walk in the wood
& nobody was to blame
& everybody was to blame
& nobody was the same
& everybody was the same
dementia deterred today

/Damn you all/

wild cooing of doves in distant branches
beyond the curtain drawn window
          in the darkened room
where he sits on the edge of the bed
frail & thin gently nodding to & fro
thinking progress be damned

                         nation states wear hoods
                  ghost riders in the sky stampede
                     the plains & piss in the oceans
                 the salmon from the rivers have gone
                    in what seas will they now spawn
                       & he is down by the riverside

down by the riverside   where
he casts his line into its waters
waiting for it to tauten   the sudden
tug   the thrill electric of connection
the flick   the jerk   as a wriggling
sparkling life   glints in the light
sails through space to land at his feet

                  the poetic stance
            oh not at all   damn you all

51

Metopes (iv)

(a series of experimental poems produced circa 2020 and mostly performed for the online venue Transforming with Poetry hosted from Leeds UK)

/Dissonance after Mallarmé/

in the me hit the in the me hit the moonlight through the pines
moonlight through the pines   moonlight through the pines
road jack a boat to pines on road jack a boat to pines on road jack
a boat to pines on
``````````````````````road jack a boat to pines on
cmon everybody
```````````````````````````````````````````yes we red sails knock
yes we  red  sails knock yes we red sails knock yes we red sails
knock
red sails in the sunset          red sails in the sunset
red sails in the sunset          red sails in the sunset
````````````````````````````````````````````knocking  on yes bye no


                    hit the road jack
bananas

                    cmon  everybody     cmon everybody
                    cmon  everybody     cmon everybody
cry bye on a slow boat to china  cry bye on a slow boat to china
slow china slow china  slow china slow china      bye bye
blackbird bye bye blackbird  bye bye blackbird bye bye blackbird
me heaven's door me heaven's door me heaven's door me heaven's
door ````````````````````````yes we have no
bananas````````````````````````yes we have no bananas        yes
we have no bananas
````````````````````````````````````````````

yes we have no bananas   knocking moonlight   knock
knock knocking knock knock knocking knock knock knocking
knock knock knocking
through the blackbird on
through the blackbird on
through the blackbird on
through the blackbird on through the blackbird on through the
blackbird on
heaven's door heaven's door heaven's door in the me hit the in the
me hit the in the me hit the in the me hit the in the me hit the
smoke gets in your eyes smoke gets in your eyes   smoke gets in
your eyes   smoke gets in your eyes

/Grasp/

grasp from bone to throat
       will warble like a flute at air
           music uttered with a gasp
& emptiness of hand
          in the space between
what must become a fist   against embedded stone clenched
clasped strikes bone
            tool tone pain the softly surfaced
            mind to map disembodied how it
              day slips beyond its grasp
                at air music uttered
              with what must become

a fist maps disembodied how it day
will warble like a flute the softly surfaced mind
to a grasp at emptiness against embedded stone
            clenched clasped to grasp from bone
           to throat hand in space between
           strikes of bone tool tone & pain
like a flute's emptiness against the embedded softly surfaced mind
              how it day will from bone to throat
hand in space grasp with what must become between
bone tool a fist   map   strikes at air
disembodied music   uttered

day marches on stilts the ground waves goodbye to tomorrow in incandescent bursts as the abyss blinks in trembling space and music flowers from pheromones a sap of words seeped in greenery whilst nothingness lingers in empathy's core together with the running order of chaos as it showers into dust clouds a shrouding abundance where *abstraction viewpoints* trickling and diaphanous evanescent landscapes

as day marches on stilts the ground waves goodbye to tomorrow and showers into dust a sap of words seeped in incandescent evanescent bursts as music flowers from pheromone clouds a shrouding abundance in landscapes where empathy's core together with abstraction viewpoints trickling and diaphanous in trembling space an *abyss blinks* in greenery whilst nothingness lingers in the running order of chaos

then showers of dust sap into evanescent waves of goodbye to tomorrow as music flowers from pheromone clouds and a day marches on stilts the ground shrouding abundance where empathy's core together words seeped in incandescent landscapes burst with abstraction viewpoints trickling and diaphanous to blink whilst *nothingness lingers* trembling space in the running order of chaos an abyss of greenery

/Slanting side show on one#two#three/

(i)

< chintz >
day of the cars   a graze of grass   sheep hedgerow
making hegemonic skyline   wires cutting clouds   wonky
dyke drive in   nettle eureka
stacks without smoke wrought iron window blurs a face in pastel
blue
day of the crane   the hill lateral   just cross over chevron bypass

the high street's as empty as the daytime
every where's empty   the outback sky   trees with no leaves
noticeable about the playground   sand   following the big black
glass   < i walk into you >   a skull in the bramble picked clean by
scavengers

every where's deserted   there's a fence between   the enclosures
blow sky don't diminish more i can scarcely keep you in
here come
                    the imaginals   watch my stick
into the -mouth- of the cave's roar
does time freeze flood or fall?   profile chewed up most of that
day of the crane   cleaver   where's it gone oh shit   rotate
                              a white   in a city through trees
skip along moonlight through the pines   hogey   nifty   hooded
                              #
that landscape's cheating on the original
repetition is not completion   ~~~~~~   coming back it 's still
deserted   day of the crane   day of the car   hood into
time spent waiting   after the bath night lights skyline scarfed
grotesque obelisks   endure on the street   no one meets

<first-one-last-one>   fame as we all know is an
illusion   day of the imaginals
hey ho the lads who went to war   the fabulous life
the impossibility of it all   on our daily Mount Moriahs

                         #God is silent

(page break)

(ii)

                         <fractals in summertime>

on the periphery primroses wild in a meadow sweet straw hat
arms akimbo   she   he munching the same cud
day of the carnival   <patterns with a dazzle>   antennae
lotus versus lilies   splatter the pane   magic again
in a sliced frame saloon interior   –   where the green abounds
wind generator harvested field fern on the way   she pirouettes
on air to the pond   day of the pond   go green at the pond
closure   white mannequins in high window   shot
                                   what follows on
she poses in a garden of roses <   > it's an unnatural end
cul de sac <   > reflection deceives water lilies   moor-hens
sunken branches in their shadows   all in their boundary layers
of surfaces drown in shine on the peripheral horizon attendant
regard non committal stares   on the edges of muddy banks
~~~~~~~~~~~~~~~~~~##
monuments   shoppers on displays by their electric coronas
ghosts mew in the park   cats stray   coffee table bird time
                                   ~ perch which-a-way
more monuments   like embalmed sweets   their shadows
carry you inside crinkly colours clipped in a mirror on a silver
stair   paper float (air) boats on the glass wall   art décor
paper refreshments   occasion in the sacrificial   accolade
save the cats   time branches from perspective to artifice
~~~~~~~~~~~~~~~~~~

(page break)

(iii)

                                                             down river //
  a glimpse instanced in a stacked stance under the bridge   cat on
the roof (black)   t   here was a plague
a multitude in pastiche   heads up everywhere   old masters
eternally retouched   where we fade   offices to let
sitting out history on the lawn's minions   between pickets of
tyranny   <as if the far side were one step>   an impossible reach
not to impossibility   but to serve only ruins   (   )
down the strands
their glittering cones of light   emptiness chimes the hour
adds a person in less than a minute
a poisoned banquet for all   the ultimate consummation
                                         bubbles surface on
                                         the day of the plague

above us only bell

                                                          no exit

from the bus stop............

                                         suddenly it's *lilac*

again
a garden of your own red in tooth & claw   round the corner
follow in fact   either the sky or us
is it a UFO or the government?

burlesque in cartoon charade   a sufficient distortion
of fact

O' Finnegan JJ yet today:
in the beginning Adam and Eve – The Fall: *of a once wall strait*
oldparr is retaled early in bed and later on life down through all
Christian minstrelsy. ... thunder in several world languages,
including French (*tonnerre*), Italian (*tuono*), Ancient Greek
(*bronte*) and Japanese (*kaminari*) – & the word was

bababadalgharaghtakamminarronnkonnbronntonnerronntuonnth
unntrovarrhounawnskawntoohoohoordenenthurnuk =

100 letters word   i agree   ugh! thunderstruck thunders
thundering forcing force forcefully generatively O Zeus
mio culpa nada on u
& do do ok not not   o ho u ouna ron   awmoghast
want got it word *abada*

bababadalgharaghtakamminarronnkonnbronntonnerronntuonnth
unntrovarrhounawnskawntoohoohoordenenthurnuk

to have read under karma number now babe ought to. break rotten
hound aka oohoo   nuke murder bang   none neuron brother
wow the thouna the better   thunder thumb bum dumb damn
garden hero never ghost   in u me them then name   run out
game murder   better (far) lonely as the rhinoceros

bababadalgharaghtakamminarronnkonnbronntonn
erronntuonnthunntrovarrhounawnskawntoohoohoordenenthurnuk

than i wander lonely as a cloud

/Mosaic/

Outward bound
harvest bales
yellow bundles

a day's heart's blaze
camouflages the human EyE

Hay fly   EyE of the fly
a pin cushion of air in spin

a darting mosaic
over
cacophony of machine
on asphalt clay

our monuments of decay

out of the absence

EyE of the fly
photoreceptorcontractor
entangling the speed of light
a mosaic out of the shadows
out of the insect & their flowers

out of the insecticide
desiccated plastic
on the rusted barbed wire fencing
shattered glass in the ditch
our pink bacteria

again again / return / tides / drifts / sands / footprints / forever /
nothing more / death / birth /kaleidoscope / dreams / appear / face
/ tapestry / weave / windswept / cries / seagulls / voices / mosaic /

i trace a mosaic / again again / as though / return / voices of the
dead / tides / on a swarm of seagulls / sands / cries across /
footprints / a windswept sea / forever / would weave / nothing
more / a tapestry /

mosaic / of a face / as though / to appear / voices / in your dreams
/ seagulls / & fragment there / cries / in a kaleidoscope /
windswept / your birth / weave / your death / fragment / nothing
more / face /

but that forever / appears / your footprints / dreams / wash in the
sands of time / kaleidoscope / on the drifts / birth / of moonlit
tides / death / to return / nothing more / forever / tides / drifts /
again again /

mosaic / as though / voices / seagulls / cries / windswept / weave /
tapestry / face / appear / dreams / kaleidoscope / birth / death /
nothing more / forever / footprints / sands / drifts / return / again
again /

/Voyeur/

voyeur
celebrant
what?

    yesterday's
    tomorrows?
    elegies for

        graveyards?
        odes o'er
        cribs

    with desert
    blue
    left in turn

by
desert hue
night & day

    carrying
    a tent
    until oasis

        befriending
        mirages
        wayside

such that
we are
the world

                              & you
                              the same
                              instant

                                             watch it
                                             disintegrate
                                             further

fringes
from
apperceptions

                         drop drop
                         dropping
                         into chasms

                                             words
                                             that tumble
                                             & clink

onto
their
echoes

                    yet
                    voyeur
                    far

                                             wherever
                                             that
                                             still is

listening
as waves
moan

       a future
        setting
         them

               free from
                the sea
                  unto

horizons
disappearing
before

       reach
      but that
       still

                define
                precipice
                  as

waiting
through
the shore

       sheer
      before
        fall

/Voices/

*like phantoms / eye to eye/ before flames / multiple voices/
cascade /appear & disappear/ in blank   incomprehension/ here /
where i hear /with my ear/ here   /   no distance / between   /
shadow play / words   / listen & listened / i see /   present &
absence / remembered / billions of people / under social systems
/ their brains / distorting echoes /   over time   / as we / pass
/ the point / of no return / her e / far away / the hill / is there
/ but still   / i can see / a place   /i'd like to be / right now / & /
i wish i were /   a bird / in the world /   i'd fly /   like a / comet /
there / so / i was reading / something / very interesting /when
/ i realised /my eyes /were closed / & when / i opened them
/ i'd no idea / where i'd left off / from before / except   / it /
had nothing to do / with what / i thought / i had / been /
reading   / which was better / i couldn't / believe it / i had /
just lost / it all / same old shit / on the window sill / i wish /
i was / a bird / & could fly / to the hill /   looking at the /
unthinkable crime /   so late / in the day / quite an   /
indescribable crime / against /   all time /   without making /
predictions / just   vaporizations   / about voices   / i hear /
there / here /*

shortage
shotdown
shutdown

      in our
      short age
      water & time

              buy
            and sell
            the sky

eat drink
& be merry
for tomorrow

     we buy

          new oil

     blue gold

            POD
           in the Hub
         & pull the plug

dip your toes
in the flow
& watch

     the money
     grow
     water water

everywhere
up for auction
like health care

in
competitive
water wealth

as you
float
on your back

in your
swimming pool
& stare

into
the unending
reach

of space
as if it were
a resource

in nature's
supermarket
to buy

& sell
the price
of life

                    drop
                  by drop
                   into

                              the algorithm
                             where we're
                            waiting in line

standing in
the queue
of shortage

                    in our
                  short age
                water & time

Metopes (v)

(in what lost presence do we really stand)

/A Quantification of Time/

fragments of the day embodied
in its wake of forgetfulness
towards an edge

a becoming   a return
an instant of the world
reaching to touch
the whole   the less

a universe that unfolds me
its solitary stranger
to greet its oncoming rush

its image left in doubt
its moment a bonfire
heap of antiquity
where insects scuttle forlorn

/Pixel/

on this pixel patch
of space
the world revolves
in a fish eye
on a painted face
pivoting
on this point of rest
on an infinitesimal
in a sea of unknowing

yellow
our salvation
our doom
goes on & off
a nebulous flux
like lights
on a Christmas tree
on a painted face

yellow

pivoting
on this point of rest
of space
on this pixel patch
life moves on
in a fish eye
the world revolves
on a painted face

in a fish eye
 pivoting
on this point of rest
of space
on this pixel patch
life moves on
on a painted face
the world revolves
yellow

 the world revolves
 our salvation
our doom
 life moves on
 on a painted face
 in a sea of unknowing
on this pixel patch
on a Christmas tree

yellow

 like lights
 a nebulous flux
 goes on & off
 on a Christmas tree
 in a sea of unknowing
 pivoting
 on an infinitesimal
on this point of rest

/Out of Range/

mauve sky   grey pine
dawn breaks   (breaks range)
out of black   ripes   (out of black)
pale blue & green (green green green)
a multitude of the unseen (out of range range range)
        chorus in the pine (as as as)
drone of traffic
closing in (closing out of range)
the leaning day
where leaning freezes
where leaning melts (leaning leaning leaning)
        out of range
a parade
like a pageantry
a pattern of events
moves as when (as when as when as when)
the arrow's flight
        disappears (out of range)

        the fragrance of dawn
breaking with it 's (breaking breaking breaking)
mirage of green (out of of of of)
trees majestic or monstrous
their litter of dead wood
like bones (bones strewn bones)
strewn ruins of the dykes
a deluge of rocks
fallen to (fallen to fallen to to to)
an overgrown tomb (out of range range range)
full a dawn moon
        fades indifferently (fades)
out of day (out of range out of range out of range)

73

/Out of Play/

Constantinople Tenochtitlan   fall
in a war of the gods it was their destiny
for the gods care nothing of the mortals
& even the gods must fall
a spot a stain in the universe the soft
world spinning a trembling balance on
the wing of a flame as the candle burns
its tip an arrow's flight   where?
what comes after before and how how
does the sun go down on this pixel patch
gallows gate he's brought through to wake

to dream our affinity our presence sensed
the sensed emulation mimicked
the context writ as the property of an event
a ghost a goat a god   a profusion of
smashed acorns on the dirt road   where
hanging bowers of canopies don't take offence
at the writ served upon them   majestic
monsters discoverers across the desert's dunes
branches wafting ribbons dulcet waving arms
flowing as if a Mayday opening onto the street
where plague roams crying bring out your dead

/Smoking Mirror/

around around
the hills surround
surround
in bottle green
forest fir (once oak)
ravelled wintry spaces
airs
hues of blue
hovering mists
clouds streaked
grey purple
as if
a smoking mirror
riddled riddled
in the glimmerings
of shadow secrets
will o'wisps
that on the texture
of this retina
may be a wave
a field evaporating
into nothingness
or here
on this balcony
earthbound
our presence presenced
in the rhythm of all things
where they say - give back
give back give back give back
back   back   back

in the transition of
the moment
the rock
speaks its voice
its echo its entropy

in the flight of life
its escape
in the obsession
of now

here in this
sway of sways
stones of an ancient world
into what breach
what chasm do we fall

 in this instance of now
as if it patrols always
an end
here there wherever
downhill
here in the musk

wafting the silence in the fern
beyond the tolling of the bell

/Underside/

a thousand green tongues
where each bespeaks each other at once
their death outlives our death
they do not fear death as we do but only us
here beneath our green sheen breathing
in what lost presence do we really stand
i want to say i have sensed your presence
but it has been taken away from me
i want to say that is my claim
as i lie in the field today where
two wide winged eagles hover high

& stand transfixed in the scene
where i ask of it why this why you
because not far away i see
the old souls of my ancestors
go over the hills
on on on out of view & i know
i can follow none of them
but i wonder if some ever found Eden
beyond our blame for where we remain

/Top O'Hill/

tree at the top of the hill   from a rooftop
a pigeon flies off over
the drone of white noise
behind you
an ephemeral mountain glides
& i wonder with you
as the crow flies
to raise my skeleton to the skies

keys wallet mobile glasses

i leave to face
the chores of our existence
whilst you lighter than air
tree at the top of the hill
are careless
whether or not there's free will

time is the darkness
where i dream of you beneath my skin
as my blood flows back to the forest
& the wind in the leaves breathes come in

forest feline fir purring
        his vagrant days that like tattered
         rags clothe his face
         as autumn leaves fall

        we walk together now to listen talk
        where both our persons are now
          diminished
          before the tempest of ice
        & fire consumes us once more

but soft ye now I will feed you with my blood

let me breathe your music as my words
already bawdy in the day
with the pantomime we play
on this our funeral day – hooray

        i care not for the molecules of kings
         nor the stratagem of regimes
        where we walk diminished in our pain

& yet I say we will regain & you

        will come again   *jaguar moon*
      forest feline purring your dawn dusk's born
    hawthorn & the rowan   the red berries growing

        a van flashes by our simulacra
        i have nothing to offer you
        but my blood in your music

beyond our most unreasonable crime

(before the human territorial voice in)
invades & after
the sun shines it's sudden shine
our end begins
     as I stumble through the straw
     but this is beech place not pine
     though i guess it's the same decline

in the end   *& the skyline rang out release me*

/Illusions/

i am watching the trees speak
opposite me in *un pueblo*
sitting on a street bench
lined in a small cluster
rough strong bark
on their trunks
about a hundred years old
shooting forth their new Spring green
imbued with a sudden joyful vigour
imparted from trunk to trunk
an intangible force challenging
the day's scenario
a vigour personified
as a joyful expression
quite unlike anything human

all in my imagination
their spoken agreement
an illusion but an illusion
we share   i tell them

/Winter Trees/

slumber keep [i roam]
wild stark ugly beauty
your deciduous hibernation
listening for your heart beat
but my ears are too faint
so slow you grow so old

& i wonder – do you dream
the world?
our lost souls SOS

do you have nightmares
things that go bump in the night?

clearance – do you dream you may never wake?

to chlorophyll green
everywhere & nowhere
nestling the life within

only the chainsaw
sawn off stumps
oozing resin

roots quivering deep beneath the terrain
to another dream lost to carboniferous origins
where the sky scorched & the ground froze
as forests burned down to an embedded tomb
where later a clever little monkey climbed down
to feast upon fossil fuels on the vanishing tree line

/Hotel Naledi/

where where O Naledi
a million years before *they* came
here   on the southern savannah
          creature of berry   wood   bone & antelope

had you always haunted
the subterranean world as a sepulchre
with your charred offerings
          and your dead   or was it just when *they* came
bigger brained with their sticks & stones

you do not often see each other
you can evade them from the plain
like you *they* roam in groups
thirty   forty   no more

                    you can hide   you can conceal
                    but sometimes come the raids
                    the raids of the *newcomers*

you twist & writhe   wriggle & crawl
on your belly on your back
through the cavernous fissures of the dark earth

                    towards your terminal chamber
                    together with your contaminated dead

so many moons have passed
more than a few centuries
but what is time on the savannah
they grow strong   you grow weak
          they are a different germ   it won't be long

83

this is your shroud
you are bound to the savannah
& *they* will go on
                    a million years will be forgotten

& now here in the Dinaledi den
we uncover your fossilised remains
we remake your skeletons
transport your mummified effigies   into our age

our brains blew up & shrank back again
though yours tiny as it was
had done as much before we came

              but perhaps ours was the disease
                that put the world to flame

Poseidon's Arse

on a northern Iberian coast
      on a north Atlantic sky
            el ceilo nublado gris
on a white wall
     from where i lay
         a little to eastwards
             a picture frame

outside there are meticulous cleaned pavements
         lined with sleek streamlined vehicles
residential shutters invite
to expensive mariscos around the corner
& steadfast back packing Santiagoers stride out

           through the skylight
         canopies of trees curiously
            part
         to display a palace
          on the horizon
through the window
light travels over
       a spread of neat
urban gardens
     with domestic palms

       to reach a peninsula creek extended in a sea
      as if by design to comfort our landscape vistas

on a white wall
a picture frame
on a white wall
within the frame

two giant stones
emerge from or descend into
the brine
as though two massive
misshapen buttocks
and
cleft between them
a night black
cavernous breach

Poseidon´s arse
wades the wine dark sea

a replication of memories
where the old becomes the new
where the world splits in two
with Morpheus in the breach

a permutation permeating the matrix of time
filters through the ages
on a mnemonic wave

on the borderland of dream
nature feels in curves
caressing a specious present
as the worlds listen
folding & unfolding
on the demiurge of time
we are thrown out
a vital spark
that sets the gods & goddesses
to flame like wild fire
at the portal of dreams
in the primordial crucible of the mind
as the horizon swims on wings

86

                    like unicorns

              nature articulates her bones
              everything has its affinity
                a series of affects
               worlds within worlds
a perspective
a point of view
becoming
its own nature
a person

gods & goddesses
                personae
                    mind but beyond mind
but still mind
                   between worlds
                    enter now
                 on a mnemonic wave
                  the wine dark sea
                the chasm upon the waters
                 unfathomable depth
                 beyond the blackness as
                   Poseidon
              moves the might of the ocean
             between the pillars of the straits

into the waters of the lagoon
in pale ephemeral light

                    where sea nymphs
                sing the song of the sirens

Dialogue with the Trees

the ghost of the forest speaks

ice melts   rivers run dry   what comes after the glaciers
north melts   south burns lungs of the world gasp heart of
the world

ebbs

blood from plant to sea
withers in the roots

any person's voice that echoes here

the forest emulates   an orchestration   a multi nature of affects
a multi nature of perspectives   a point of view becomes a
person   flesh enters the forest   a lovers embrace
a consummation

as well as

the phantom predator
in the shadows lurks
as its prey stalks the sky

sky wind & leaves poised   to

forest and sea breathe   the nature of nature   a history of ice
and fire   stars collapse   suns burn out   black holes bounce
super novas explode   planets implode   churned through the
mill of existence   to spawn a molecule of life   an instant in
infinity   a quantum of eternity

echoes

as the forest of the universe
tumbles into metamorphosis
O flesh
what is the nature of nature

then O jaguar moon come

stand push pull lift press (proprioceptive)   stillness stills on
the jaguar moon   on the soft prowling night   paw padded
through the stars   in your eyes   the forest's lustre glows moon
mind   running sleek as night   upon the shores bounding
break   as you leap between   us through us   jaguar moon
by the waters we listen   to your feet on these same

same

shores where we meet open
sky fall sky open sky fall sky
in the many mingling throng

90

in the many mingling throng we come

time paints the sky beneath the skin   we begin in the furthest
star   that blinks in the heart of the forest (here)   where   (i)
stand still with time   wherever it blows   the ice age
comes   the ice age goes   we rise we fall   over with the

together with sky

we the malignant we   the magnificent munificence

chorus to the mingling throng it does

they have built their concrete jungles   on sand   we follow
led on our brain   your brain   there is no final moment
in the dust

thus spoke the tree

even as the planet
fades we knew you from before you
came that you cannot know us more

an outlaw's forest's berserk voices   /

where is your woo(r)(l)d – va(r)nished   wilderness is a truth
you cannot share   the scorched desert   the arctic waste   we
did not understand   you'd been driven back on the line   our
oracles   do you remember them at all   i'll give

i'll go now & ask for your return

to return my heart to the jaguar moon
nature is both in her entangled state
from the wilderness to the wilderness
I summon you my children's children

an oracle to the conference of persons thus spoke

you are but a semblance   at flow in your blood   which   is
your end   your rot is not as ours   let us capture your
semblance   in our resemblance   & we will return you   to
the stars like the rain & the wind we bespeak   we are your

underworld your overworld

you pass between us
either as a shade
or as a living breath of blood

92

a trace of Sapiens

O forest long ago   we cut out your   ancient heart & burnt
it at the stake & built a timber fort   as we rafted with you across
the seas   & cast you down

stream to the mill

*where's 'el refugio' for us
in the nooks & crannies
after the apocalypse?*

a poet interrupts to ph(r)ase in

three pigeons   play in the twigs   of a swaying bough   as if in
embrace   saccades entangle   time leaps   time bounces

seen

*from afar a solitary blackbird
waves to & fro on a high
branch extending into the sky
do not fear – but do fear
the human dart to your heart*

on the borderline wending you came blending

winding in   down by the meer   next to the fencing   the
fenced in fencing   down by the border line   the meer   next to
the green   the fenced in   fenced off green   down by the
meer   who

a few centuries after

our disappearance
nature would leave
few vestiges of human civilisation
in a million years only a wafer thin fossil

the great wall of China   perhaps a final remnant
would probably be covered

in lichen & fungi with only   the head of the Dragon   in the
sea   its back in the mountains   & its tail in the desert
/ i wish /   i was /

94

the ghost of the forest speaks

heaven reflects   the surface of all things   and the forest breathes
life into the ocean   the forest of the sea bleeds   but does not
breathe   the forest of the earth   breathes but does not bleed

**O blood heart beat the roll of the drum   the rumble of
thunder**

*our roots veins run into earth
entangle with the mycelium
entangle but also strangle
the ocean*

dialogue with the trees

we withstand the fury of the elements

                              spring dazzles

as if a tabula rasa

95

we are their catharsis   their

metamorphosis   even time is a wanderer   that returns to
the forest   we burn   we freeze   we drink   we bleed
we harvest death & shriek aloud at it   you are ours who make
believe   all else is mockery

experience as young

*experience as old
it's not the same   it's a
random number   lost even to itself*

everything struggles without purpose

the only purpose that exists   is   to share the abundance of the
moment   which is lost again and again   which returns
again and again   perhaps for you   there is a oneness   to the
moment in its abundance   but it is not really so   everything
has its absolute limit   its inexorable finitude   time is only
the forest   there is no such thing as perfection   we eat nature
nature eats us   praise be to the jaguar moon

the spirits of the dead are in your roots

*you clone the world but what alikes
the like of an orchestration
its nature of nature
its point of view*

**the meadow and the pack   the owl's screech   the predator
and the prey**

the pulse of the planet   what choice   what chance   time
swoops arrival after its departure   entangled in a moment
the lichen devours the rock   the forest transforms the lichen
& we summon the spin of the planet in a swirl of galaxies to feed
a star   our pigmentation paints the maps of eternity   here in the
core   our proprioceptive presence

saccades alight

*in mirages that evaporate
only to reappear   hauntings in a veil of
memories   beckonings and belongings*

we emulate

through the seasons time's becoming   time is the forest and it's
wanderer therein

on this

*pixel patch of existence
spring dazzles as if a tabula rasa
praise be to the jaguar moon*

Rhythms of Existence

Fragments of Eden in Broken Bonds

a glimmer flashes beneath the threshold
> *eye of the gannet*

in folded wing dives sheer in flight
> *Mast at Bass Rock*
>> *white feathers cheek by jowl*
>> *putrefy*
> it will not go away

once upon a time
a wild duck came
to a mill pond
where a hen pecked
& a pig chomped

> ***& an ape smoked its pipe***
>> *in a world of flame*
>> *money frames*
>> *the arm's game*

> ***where are you hidden O Eden***

> transcendental anthropocentrism
>> assumes
>>> cartoon simulation

then
run with the ***Jaguar Moon***
from the anthropocene
> **& the age of the sixth**
> **extinction** has come & gone
>> *to where the cascade of life*
>> *resumes its growth*
>> *noble savage*
> *until a new age of homo sapiens*

Metamorphosis

A surge on the wave
breaks to spray
turbulence becomes a vortex
do the spiral galaxies dream
here in the helix of my heart

new patterns appear in rhythm
worlds within worlds
a mirage wherein quivers a trace
elements that assume intent
an event transitioned into now

into metamorphosis a demiurge
where fury of fire flood quake
drought or rage of apocalypse
or us between
a nebulous symbiotic moment

as nature in its rags & glory roams
its own wilderness lost & found
as life flows on
in eternal metamorphosis

TheTrance of the Bat

wayward in its way strays
the intangible nebulous thought
across evanescent landscapes
like a spider in a web
haunting a void
from which it cannot escape
but to a shape
thought like a bat in the dusk
flutters in the abyss
of the thought made word

the forest we come from
and the forest we return to

a dance closer than touch
where even our fragmentary words
resonate with its pulsation
its cascade through the forest of dreams
in its orchestration of existence
where dancer & dance become one

Beluga

white dolphin without wing

homing   drawing succor beneath the ice floe

*where the river meets the sea
downstream from the forest
song of the ocean a sonic alphabet
a web of sound we have yet to know*

moving northward with nowhere to go
until the gulf of mexico
here today   gone tomorrow

your palace of ice

i listen now for your call lost to us

still i am here upon the shore

*or perhaps you outlive us all
deep upon the sea bed's eddies
don't you already know? we listen
but do not understand at all*

in those warm seas where you might roam
who is the predator & who is the prey?

beyond our simulation
our simulacra
our Anthropocene

Laminations in Lacquer

In a bright lit night, he lays his bed deep in hues of Lapis Lazuli.
In the corners sit the winds dressed like musical chairs.
An olive ferments in a pastel saucer into mossy green minutiae
where a painted flower swallows against its form, liquid spaces
in lean reflections towards a bottomless well.

Veils swim on the verge the flower defines
drawn against an olive splash of skin
in the glazed lacquer
gloss to the anonymous images.

A cock crows cockle doodle do discrete, concrete,
on the fronds
ruffles in the red sprocketed throat
a screech of feathers stilled in the flowers passion
in the pool's hoard.

The gibbous mound, a crimson flash in the curtain
through which he passes beneath the bridges.
A stairway in pastel hue laps tranquilly cool
to a hole in a wall
a cavernous breach which retains
the scream of the arch scrawled on a screen
defiant in the stance of plumages,
hordes of epiphanies buried in petrified pastel ripples.

Below the rift of its eye
the sealed beak that will open
gleams on the lee.

Throughout the entire circumference
can be seen the tilt giving rise
to both translucence, transparency,
where the acid, oil separate
only to appear to coalesce
in the almost pure liquid sheen
containing its own light
even in the presence of the vegetative
silt at the bottom of the bowl.

At the moment of its brimming
at that line of definition
in a room that roams without corners
he must rise with a chalice of blood for lips of shades
where the vertigo edge of the flower distills the dish
together with the quantities of immeasurable throng
on watery groves billowing with ivy bowers
sprung over hidden lairs of concealed hoards.
Night begins and the dogs draw nigh
scavenging for scraps yapping at the walker's naked ankles
in the dust of unknown allies.

The broken lights of the bazaar spangle with glittering promises,
the eyes of the dusky beggar sunk in their sockets maze
in crooked cul de sacs embargo amidst the furls of silk that foil
the flickering lantern niche throttled in an olive tray,
whilst the flower's blur does not allow
the stroke that blurs its horizon
and all beneath to return.

It is helpless in its light a camouflage to visitation
to the sigh of the rock's flow so few, so few, so few.

The olive saturates its wish
outlining monuments amidst the rubble
in momentary musical explosions
and the spell is cast.
Fireworks like a diaphanous lithograph print an emblazoned sky
on the craggy mountains of the night where comets play at kites
& glistening the eerie beak hisses...

Rhythms of Existence

time moves from fast to slow
in these extremes
from flow to still from still to flow
you want to know in the sub lunar
region where you're born
the rhythm of the coming dawn

a rhythm that translates
on the turn of a horizon
into what comes after that horizon
on the whirlpools of time

mortal immortals
immortal mortals
living each other's death
*dying each other's life**

in gesture & imitation
to the rhythms of existence

*** Heraclitus**

The Triumph of the Left Hemisphere (i)

cobwebbed her face spun the spell of lechery a garden of forked
paths   day and night tremble on the morning and evening star
morning brings the gull's squall surreal beyond the curtained
windows   the trees are ivy clad in a laurel bay like ship mast &
rigging sunk to the bottom of the sea

a filament of silver stabs the heart a slumbering breast cloud
blooded in night's music on no breath of breeze
& flesh on flame trembles beneath naked branches
churlish fetching as though milk maids were wenching
like little red riding hoods
nor no kiss can seal our wound to heal not her him
him her not I nor mine

Godlike creation must be seen as producing monsters
in the gilt mirror of crooked butterflies where paper boats float
with gondoliers beneath its arches and children drown
in innocence of the first reflected face
new ice age melts into soft ultra violet great maws devouring
fleece ascend the statues of the sky towards melting blue
a sky in chains Atlantic winds mast banners
wave musk of weed overgrown graves

paper castles on glass tables doll house tombs
golden curls & dimples
from ghost houses screams the jackal down the long white hall
down the long white mall
city of bleach close to the wind's white corners
ballerina in a champagne glass cherry lips
sparkling eyes golden hair

107

delicate toes in bubbling foam until the last sips
disappear in ripples
a pink & white cloud mattress washed
to pillows of bleached stone
crepe clouds plume a three cornered hat pistols bloom back roses

The Triumph of the Left Hemisphere (ii)

the first line on the page thought to escape its life sentence
like an errant angel falling into the breach
a heavenly ape descended & disappeared into the waters
transfixed the statue wears the same mask as the crowd transfixed
heaven & hell are on the spin of a coin
blue whales' melodies turned to shrieks are the ocean's voice
& the iceman cometh to explain the glory of a name
by which he would be forgotten

write thin rice words to the roll of rice drums
give alms to blindness
papyrus on a brain stem in a ventilation shaft
rivers of red ink we scratch fears of the trembling vertebrate
the long field shrew fleeing the hill to frozen waste
rice burning the paper sky
small bones in the stubble frail nib at the edge
forlorn the streets we drift we drift
on waste on waste no fiesta for the poet
no poem for the feast walk down
walk down the western lane take heed
the locusts come take heed
the rice fields are burning on west on west

as string tautens bow stretches arrow pivots arcs
the long day crane drops its breaking neck
everyone imprisons in the telescope

a bleached pine branch floats its sodden joint wrenched
first came fresh in sweet pods & green mush splitting on
black lips black omnipotent tongue
heart's red blood trickling to feed gorilla sky rains
cockroaches singing in the rain all the milk white spilt heaven
coquette ruffles & coiffed wigette
wrought in cream meringue ostrich plumes

& the newsman comes on measure of all things
who rose from the glaciers
first dialectical of an interlocutor to a third person
in hypothetical argumentation of an imaginary plot
fallen man in a museum in narrow straights
in the gallery on the knoll
moulds without holds different helmets in the battle
black out at the shootout banquets in display of poison bouquets
thaws to time's articulated perception
a line with no other representation but its manifold variation
the mirror is all fur through trees convoluted branches
whose littered scales spangle downwind their voices

The Triumph of the Left Hemisphere (iii)

                                    mother of god in the death pen
she's dancing on a string a marionette at the gallows she sings as
she swings one big world yes on everybody's lips her mouth
stains the mirror with a kiss after the eight fold city of light
the morning hymn on high where the dragon fly pays homage to
the lotus to fame with Mozart in another room from another room
with another name on the radio made in china drift like a broken
antler in the soft silt quick on the swivel still unslacking raging
silent till torn aloft close your eyes

                                        on your borders for now it's
safe to dream & awake from a parallel dream of unknown
separation where you reach out before
bandaged banisters spiral as a monstrous thorax
throttled on each gargantuan gargoyle floor
a white electric cell stormed in the head of a whale that flounders
crashes onto the street of harlot shouts to become a reed at dawn
kept by the river of day & night kept by the sea in a window
where the raven shrieks dressed like a black flamenco
& every one spills in the shapeless sky

                                        shedding rags in pirouettes
dark shards piercing the sunset in proportion to gravitation
yet they whispered she knew not she only her beloved called
on lonely raven ridges still her icy wails flail on bitter winds
not freedom from your rags raised to riches by the coolies
among those dark satanic mills a shadow slithers crankily
down funicular stairs onto trap door landings & narrow long
doors through high thin halls like a crooked shank pin out in
black satin gold buckles on

                                        Nantacas seven seas Rip Van
Winkle's away to hoods on the wharves manacled bicycles in
interminable rows implore the shore's deserted canals a town's
tier walls stained in moss fungi lichen grime belies their fragrance
drain pipes in rain wild weed corners dandelion leaf red bramble
in black warts rain runs as blood into shadows its speechless
phantoms amazed after so long still misunderstood in shadowy
strands thin bands like the oneness of ant waves or piranhas
long gone dance in the womb of incubation a well of gravity that
spawns the ocean's unleashed shoal still trembling from the deeps
where you hover in suspense

Titles for Hearts

frozen tears in the breeze
as years fold like strangers
shaking hands with shadows
always sought
yet never released
hollow
as wind in the reeds
on parade
as daybreak brings
all will be as before
the covered furniture in the room

phantom ancestors of the womb
spectral
waiting
as echoes do in mirrors
we come not to the feast
but riding on the beast
or is it really so
our ancestors wait in the valley
wait in the wind
waiting to give titles for hearts

Speak to the World

speak to the world
let the world speak
to you
aiya eeya yaai yaee yai
aiya eeya yaai yaee yai
       yayu
by the tree by the fern
the hillside down
the wide wing cry
by the flash tumbled stream .
the water weir swell
by the outside in
the hidden in within
speak to the world
let the world speak
to you
aiya eeya yaai yaee yai
aiya eeya yaai yaee yai
       yayu
unfold on the brow swept
swept brow unto yonder flow
blow prayer blow
wind come wind go
day in day out sun moon
word whisper abide beside
the thin edge tone intone
speak to the world
let the world speak
to you
aiya eeya yaai yaee yai
aiya eeya yaai yaee yai
       yayu

The Grief of the Dead

i heard a voice in the forest ask since
nature spawned us & we were born to life
where have the dead gone
whose absence presences their return
embedded now in these evanescent
landscapes of the mind
this milieu of memory's membranes
to a sudden touch of dream
as if to open onto another shore
the dead who reside within my head since
the dawn of creation the dinosaur & extinction

i thálassa i thálassa mono i thálassa

as earth mutates mycelium every life form
transforms into another relation transits
to another domain & you our spectral dead
whose phantoms haunt the shores of our dismay
forget us not who are left behind
for here we are pierced
can you not redeem us your bondage
what binds you always to fade our reach
shadows who cry out beyond all vengeance
to declare you still belong amongst us

*

113

& I heard this reply
we the dead are the children of the forest
& the forest in which you are born
all life forms that have ever been
exist as mind in its infinite possibilities
as multifaceted nature
which continues in metamorphosis for eternity
what exists for us after death biological or elemental
is an infinite network of relations in the process of becoming
no possessions rule us nor judgments bequeath us
our gain is the momentary oneness of abundance
our loss is the patience to wait for it to come again
herein we visit you for you are our only grief.

The Fan

a few short years
a few short days
a few short hours
a few short moments

you (?)

beyond the exalted reach
who are you now
beyond it all
beyond its silent call
the all in all
that totalises the now
yet fragments as a peacock's fan
sailing beyond reach
beyond touch
like a rare butterfly in a jar
the prosaic word burns within a tower
whilst the rest of the world gives
and who is the world
i ask of the flower
me she sings
i am the daughter
i am the hour

Killer
(the decolonisation of occidental thought)

kill kill kill the brightly plumaged avian cackles
its bead eye gleams from its perch malevolently
somewhere deep in the heart of an ancestral tomb
a sacrificial knife is drawn over a jugular vein

and the sky is a crimson embrace

O murderer raving at the moon caught betwixt
your tanist shadow which the gods will devour
as fleshly remnants clung to your phantom soul
until your roam beyond the land of many colours

Across the Page

A million miracles
in the mystery of the moment
or a million mysteries
in the miracle of the moment
in this breath of life
this kiss of flesh made word
i scrawl across the page
as trees talk
walk
the aons of day & night
in unfathomable empathy
in unfathomable entelechy
as their patience transcends
my wandering mind
or gathers it into
abundant green fields
flowing
where the pigeon soars

Rooftops

the tiles on the adjacent rooftops
are like half cleaven flower pots
encrusted with lichen
& scattered herbaceous growth
almost bleached in sunlight
red bricks   blue sky   white clouds
& chimney stacks with flower pot
wind breakers   green guttering leads
to a drainpipe drop on a white wall
next to stone worn doorsteps
all together with the doppler traffic drone
skeletal TV ariels & a fly in the window

is anybody home
where am i now in the mind's eye

Last Tango in Paris
the rest is silence
til all the seas gang dry
and the rocks melt in the sun
Grishkin is a marionette
in the noonday sun
have you ever seen the rain

Indra's net

the tiles on the rooftops
& the red brick wall....

Reverberate

                                        on the other side

murder most foul   evil
                                        is an ontological primitive

some leeway perhaps for goodness beauty & truth
but   evil
                                        that's a human property

it's been that way as long as i can remember
so when the immortals say   we want to come down
                                      but need blood to do so
                                      blood is what flows
& my shadow reverberates   or is it already
                                      too late

for it seems the Gods
those that are nameable at least   are at war again
saturating themselves with our carnage
                                    murder most foul say i
not so say they
for that which you have bled   but the immortals have fled
                                    to the dead

i am a duck & live in a quack
as i peer through the lattice of your eye

                                    amidst the mass merger
                                    of mixed mental antagonisms
                                    in their solitary limbo
strident fetish voices of leadership
                abysmally loom the mammoth
                                    nation state political machine
to legislate their divinity
over the automata of our existence

                              but ducks can soar vertically
                              from ponds to above the tree

tops

when the shriek owl
                    swoops
                           in the dead of night
onto a soft & furry prey
                         foraging in undergrowth
                                  & tears its gut with its claw
& rips its heart out with its beak
                           where does that terrified squeak
                                  resonate in the abyss of creation
you tell me it's God getting to know itself better
                              i say process is a demiurge
                                     & we're all in it together

Gesture

In repetition of the dance
            the world we make unfolds
its secrecy for the beholder
            to see through

& enhance the allusion of a thing
            such as a world
that suddenly inhabited sees through
                        you

& the world we make
does it have hands?

say the world we make
            has hands but we hold
            the guns

& the world we make
            does it gesture
say it gestures the thought
            of whole & part
& its center is the heart

                        & ours is the fame
            whose name is blame

asleep i find i dream your heartbeat in mine
& waking find i hear the pounding tom tom
a drumbeat reverberating over continents of time
before gods & goddesses came with their acclaim
of sun & moon which they cast to stone & tomb
& after the bomb that had pulverised us to a dust
as a shadow frame from where before we'd been
across the plains of existence i hear the pulsation
resonate the rhythm in yours & mine as the same
as asleep i find i dream your heartbeat in mine
& waking find the air upon my skin breathing